Copyright © 2024 by Samantha Drobac

All rights reserved. Written permission must be granted by the copyright owner prior to using any of its content.

Book illustrations by Samantha Drobac

ISBN: 9798320872889 (paperback)

Imprint: Independently published

To my children

Author's foreword

As we know, human memory can falter over time, leading to the potential decay of many valuable memories, thoughts, and ideas. To counteract this, it proves beneficial to maintain objective records. Therefore, I bring forth a collection of a few concise essays I've authored over time. Reflections that have helped me navigate life's difficulties. In addition to this, I've collected what I consider to be wise and highly helpful contemplations by others which I will scatter throughout the book.

I believe there are valuable insights to be gained from the experiences of others. While there is no substitute for firsthand experience, learning from others can help us fill in gaps and gain clarity on our own experiences. I often think about the individuals who possessed valuable lessons to share but departed from this world before we had the chance to learn from them.

Within me reside countless thoughts and observations that I have felt compelled to share with a wider audience. Sadly, my perfectionist inclinations led me to wait for the perfect alignment of external circumstances or the acquisition of more knowledge and experience before I could share. However, a pivotal moment occurred when I had a dream in which I found myself on the brink of death, with only a few minutes to spare. And in those last moments, an overwhelming regret consumed me— regret for having missed the opportunity to write this book. It had dawned on me that I would be departing from this world without leaving tangible words for my children that encapsulated several important lessons I acquired from my life's journey. *"What a waste"*, I thought, and one that was overshadowed by such deep sadness since I noticed how much time I had wasted, in vain really, always waiting for the perfect moment. Therefore, my primary motivation for embarking on this endeavor comes from my children. They inspired me to create this, which I intend to leave as a lasting literary legacy for them. My hope is that this book will offer them something to hold onto and can revisit whenever the need arises.

Furthermore, it will become noticeable that the structure of my work follows its own path and not one that is usually seen in the traditional methods of writing that many are accustomed to. Everything I share, somehow all comes together in my mind, and I will do my best to explain it as clearly as possible with minimal deviation.

Also, given that we humans tend to perceive life through a primarily dualistic lens— a dichotomy that we are all familiar with and manifests in various forms: right and wrong, up and down, left and right, yin and yang, heaven and hell, and so on... Whether this principle is artificially constructed or naturally occurring is irrelevant, at least it is in this context. Ultimately, it seems that most individuals agree and are comfortable with this framework, myself included. Based on this, I have structured this book into two parts. The initial section adopts a micro-view, or zooming in, delving into intricacies, subsequently transitioning to a macro-perspective, or zooming out. Each perspective offers its distinct insights, yet both are equally valuable.

Many questions might, or will, arise as you read through my thoughts, but I hope that as the book unfolds, it all becomes clearer and is able to tackle all potential questions or doubts, ultimately presenting a cohesive and comprehensive "bigger picture".

Lastly, intellectual humility is something I've been diligently practicing for many years. Rather than immediately dismissing ideas, concepts, or hypotheses, I strive to keep an open mind. I take the time to genuinely consider the potential and validity of each situation. For instance, I often engage in thought-experiments where I challenge my own ideas, thoughts, and beliefs to assess their strength and validity, while being open to accepting when they happen to fall short of my expectations. This practice is crucial for fostering mental flexibility and avoiding rigid and/or linear thinking. Continuously nurturing intellectual humility means staying open to possibilities and recognizing that we don't know all there is to know, as well as we don't know what we don't know. That being said…three important things need to be considered prior to reading the thoughts I've written in this book: (i) keep an open mind, (ii) everything I've written here is open to question; nothing I say is ever conclusive or absolute, and lastly, (iii) as a great guru master, Ram Dass, once said: *"take what you need and let the rest fall through you like Chinese food"*.

Happy reading.

"In the theater of the soul, a tale unfolds,
Where mind and heart, their stories told.

In the crates of the mind, a sauce so sly,
Causing pain, a hurt, a clever lie.
An innocent trick, though not meant to harm,
The heart entangled, in the mind's charm.

Innocence dances in this intricate game,
As the heart embraces the mind's clever flame.
Yet, pain may linger in the heart's embrace,
A trick played out, a moment's grace.

But behold the wisdom, deep within,
The heart's sanctuary, where truths begin.
A force much stronger than the mind's charade,
Prevails in moments witty tricks fade.

For the heart's guidance, a beacon bright,
Shines through the shadows of the mind's night.
In times of need, the mind will seek,
The wisdom of the heart, humble and meek.

The mind, entangled in its web so smart,
Turns to the heart for a fresh start.
Falsehoods and jests, once veiled in play,
Discover solace in the heart's gentle sway."

Black & White

It's fascinating how particular types of questions can prompt specific responses, whereas entirely different inquiries will yield their own answers. Each question holds the potential to lead us down entirely unique paths in our quest for understanding. Therefore, it's crucial to know which questions to ask, especially when attempting to comprehend aspects of human nature. But as we know, no single question exists that can yield an absolute answer that encapsulates the entirety of many existing whys, whats and hows. As multifaceted as we are, we've managed to comprehend and measure certain aspects of ourselves as far as our senses and technology permit, but others might forever remain enigmatic to us, resisting the degree of understanding we long for no matter how deeply we delve into it.

In our pursuit to get a better grasp of what we as humans are about, we generate numerous disciplines or schools of thought to help us navigate the complicated, and what seem endless, features of humans and our relationship to life/existence— I like to envision this as branches extending from a tree. Science and mysticism[1] appear to be the primary domains from which numerous branches then extend and evolve, gradually thinning until they reach their limit. For instance, science contains several branches that extend from it rather immediately, such as physics, biology, astronomy, chemistry, and so on… If we delve into the branch that deals with physics, we will find it leads to more branches such as thermodynamics, classical mechanics, quantum mechanics, relativity… and it continues, each branch becoming narrower while simultaneously specializing deeper into certain aspects of our life.

[1. "Mysticism" seemed more suitable than "religion", since, I believe, encompasses a wider range of branches.]

    We usually align ourselves behind one of these two main domains [science – mysticism (spirituality, astrology, religion)] finding solace even if we don't endorse every subsequent subbranch or layer that falls underneath it.

    It's mostly the case that people will see science and mysticism as two conflicting disciplines, but I've usually been uninterested in joining that debate or attempting to transform these two opposites from adversaries to allies. My approach has generally been to keep it peacefully simple and merely extract what is beneficial from each one without favoring one over the other. Since I see the utility and value in both, I have tended to navigate my existence by walking with one foot in one discipline and one in the other as much as possible.

In any case, as great judges that we are— or we think we are —we should strive to refrain from seeing science and mysticism as competitors to determine superiority or correctness. Instead, we should see them as a direct representation of our human capacities for logic and emotion; reason and intuition – one helps explain the tangible facets of existence, while the other delves into the realms of the ineffable. Maybe in the future, society will undergo a transformation where it realizes that these two opposing "worlds", which have long been seen as adversaries, will come to understand that their differences are instead a single and inseparable unit.

I recognize that the thoughts in our minds can become quite vocal and assertive with their compellingly logical arguments that tend to overshadow the heart's insights due to the heart's much subtle delivery, but if we cannot, or won't allow, ourselves to hear both sides we will perpetually get a dish half full.

Part One

Standing Close

Chapter I. Pain and Suffering

Suffering, being as common as we've noticed it to be, we have accepted it as part of life, but is it [suffering] necessary?

Can something as predominant as suffering, an aspect that seems almost fundamental to experiencing human life at its maximum capacity, ever possibly be deemed as "unnecessary"? It is hard, at least for me, to draw a conclusion from a world I've never known; a world without suffering.

We often fall for the presumption that a world without suffering would result in its direct opposite: a world of happiness and joy. Say this is the case, do humans even possess the capability to sustain such a world? From what I've noticed, we [humans] are unique in our tendency to cause unnecessary suffering onto others, sometimes in remarkably foolish and excessive amounts.

I should perhaps clarify that when I mention suffering from pain, I'm not referring to the typical pain or discomfort resulting from an injury or the sort that comes from daily stressors, which can be a constructive source of motivation and healthy in moderate amounts. The suffering I am addressing in this chapter is of a different nature and happens to be very influential in many aspects of our lives.

I realize this is a heavy subject to begin with. However, I opted for this because pain and suffering cross our paths quite often, even when we make every effort to avoid them. Happiness, on the other hand, doesn't appear to be as universally accessible, even though this is not entirely accurate. But also, aren't our daily routines primarily shaped by our interaction with suffering—either by trying to avoid it or seeking liberation from it? Then again, one could oppose, just as Sigmund Freud would with his *"pleasure principle"*[1] and say that our daily habits are centered on the pursuit of *pleasure* or the preservation of it when it emerges.

> 1. Freud's pleasure principle explains that our biggest motivation is the search for instant gratification either through our basic needs and/or our "primitive urges".

Nevertheless, the fear of suffering appears to always be lurking in one way or another. We would perhaps settle with a neutral state— not joyful but at least not suffering— even then, we don't wish to remain in this vegetative state for too long either because that's not living.

One day, while touring a museum, I came up to a prehistoric scene that depicted the life of a man and a woman living together in what seemed like some sort of Mesolithic hut. I took a moment to stare at them and their surroundings. The woman was kneeling on the dirt inside their hut preparing food, while the man was entering carrying wood in his arms. As I observed the scene, I wondered: *"Did our early ancestors deal with the same emotional distress as the ones we experience now? What did they argue about back then? Would there be disagreements over whose turn it was to hunt for food that day or gather wood?"*.

Their life, I believe, was very similar to animals— simple in terms of emotions yet marked by the challenges of meeting survival needs. However, as human intelligence evolved and we became cleverer, this progress carried the cost of heightened sensitivity to our own minds. With our growing intellect, our ability to enhance the pleasure of experiences increased proportionally to our capacity to experience more profound pain. In what way did evolution go so wrong? Or did it?

I've maintained the belief that suffering is indispensable for personal growth and the attainment of profound meaning. My deep curiosity about pain and suffering usually leaves others puzzled, which in turn has made me feel the need to elaborate on my reasoning in the hopes of fostering understanding. Their argument has usually been of the sort that does not see suffering as a necessary tool for growth, that one should be able to still grow and learn important lessons without the experience of suffering. I will share my thoughts on this matter as the chapter unfolds.

Pain, as we know, is an essential component for survival by alerting us when something is wrong so it can be addressed. But besides its biological utility, it occasionally holds an intriguing form of pleasure. For instance, some gain satisfaction from the discomfort of getting a tattoo, or the odd gratification behind a painfully spicy dish.

It's been proposed that the same brain circuitry that responds to pain is the same circuitry that also responds to pleasure, existing on a "continuum". I found this fascinating since it could shed light on the reason why experiences that bring pain might also carry an undertone of pleasure or the other way around such as loving someone so much that it hurt.

Now, not all pain is created equal. Lesser degrees of pain can exist in isolation, either as pure physical discomfort without any emotional distress, or vice versa. Also, it is not typically the case that physical pain prompts self-analysis and the evaluation of the legitimacy of invading thoughts. Instead, it is usually *emotional pain* that calls for that introspective direction, though not many will take that call and thus miss the opportunity to realize how that emotional pain could be revealing where we cling psychologically.

Returning to physical pain… We are quick to grasp its association with the law of cause and effect without extensive inquiry. For example, if we stub our toe on a table corner, we don't engage in deep psychological analysis. Instead, we acknowledge the cause, allow it to diminish, and proceed forward without the emotional entanglements, but perhaps just adopting preventive measures for the future. However, what is it about emotional pain that leaves us unable to apply this same method?

Also, at what point does our pain turn into full-blown suffering? I recognize that emotions in general are hard to quantify, let alone impose a boundary. Since the previous question has no definitive answer, I instead attempted to form a mental image of what pain might be in order to get a better understanding of what suffering is or where these two [pain and suffering] might meet. Not surprisingly, the more I thought about this, the more complex the visual became.

I envisioned an inner realm reserved for the experience of pain.[2] This personal domain varies in size, per se, from one individual to another, dictated by each person's unique pain tolerance [refer to Diathesis-Stress Model[3] for the psychological/emotional aspects]. Within this domain, we experience pain either from physical injury or emotional distress. As the pain persists and approaches our maximum pain threshold (the boundary of the pain domain), we stand at the crossroads of two divergent paths. One leads into the *realm of suffering*, while the other invites entry into the *realm of acceptance*. The path we tread from there on, whether towards suffering or acceptance may, or may not, be within our control—an aspect I'll touch on later in this book.

Before I delve deeper, I want to interject by adding a thought based on the previously mentioned paths: the road of suffering and the road of acceptance. It's important to clarify that acceptance does not imply an absence of suffering; in other words, that our pain and suffering will magically disappear. Instead, acceptance is about genuinely embracing our current circumstances— where we're at— without harboring resentment or bitterness, and I know that this may be hard to believe, but from what I've noticed, it's when we resist acceptance that we subject ourselves to unnecessary, prolonged, and intensified states of suffering.

2. *I do caution and warn at attempting to confine a concept such as pain, not only because accurately determining the existence of a limit is challenging but also due to the numerous complexities we must consider, including those beyond our awareness due to a lack of information or understanding.*
3. *Diathesis-Sress Model—a term used in the field of Psychology that helps explain the differences in reaction to life stressors. Considering a person's genetic predisposition (nature), combined with their environment (nurture) in the development of psychological disorders.*

Maybe suffering always occurs to some degree in the presence of any type of pain –and not just when the pain reaches a certain threshold— and the level of suffering depends on the intensity of the pain. Nevertheless, as we've noticed, specific experiences can have a lasting psychological impact, leading to prolonged suffering. This is especially the case when the experience catches us unexpectedly.

Painful experiences bring out the human in us, shining light on our fragilities but also illuminating the spots where our adaptability falls short of expectation such as when we've felt great fear that leads us to make unwise choices that we later regretted, or in the cases where we've been unable to exercise self-control in the face of something highly pleasurable, leading us to indulge, or overindulge, only to find us feeling guilty later.

Additionally, some of these situations can showcase our inherent ability to make matters worse rather than better; where we create our own mess and chaos either from negligence, naivety, or selfishness. Another more shocking situation is when pain is inflicted onto us by witnessing the magnitude of life's unpredictable nature such as by robbing us of precious company, leaving us feeling disoriented and struggling to regain internal equilibrium. Equally significant is the recognition of how prevalent malevolence is in our world, perpetuated by individuals much like us: other fellow humans—prompting the question: *"How could humans do such a thing?"*. In a general sense, suffering can remind us of our individual weak spots as well as the collective shortcomings inherent in humanity.

In any case, we notice the strong effects negative experiences have on us at such a deep level while, curiously, enjoyable experiences often appear to exhibit a strong susceptibility to fading over time, making it challenging to recreate the initial positive emotional impact in the future. While we may hold onto a sense of affection and, in some instances, even idolize specific pleasant moments or individuals, the original intensity of the experience tends to diminish substantially. Sadly, this has been the usual tendency for us: to focus, dwell, or remember more frequently the negative experiences of life and not so much the positive ones, because as clinical psychologist, Jordan B. Peterson, brilliantly put it: *"You can be completely dead, but you can only be so happy"*. In other words, our inclination towards giving more significance to negative experiences is rooted in the fact that they have the potential to lead to death. Happiness, on the other hand, can only extend so far, implying that the impact of positive experiences may be more limited (unless you're having a full-blown manic episode). Because is there something beyond happiness? No… one cannot cease to exist due to an abundance of joy. But depression? Yes, that can open the gates to places that put any human's life at risk if it gets out of hand, not only that; there are immense amount of opportunities for depression to develop.

Moving on…

Say we enter the realm of suffering. I believe we are meant to experience this [suffering], though not to remain stuck in it. This realm can swallow us whole very quickly, giving rise to trauma— where suffering becomes our personal hell. Even though there's truth to Seneca's words: *"We suffer more often in imagination than in reality"*, our imagination is intensely real to us at such moments, perhaps even more real than actual reality. It's a realm where the thoughts we compulsively replay in our minds, intending to protect us, paradoxically drive us toward the brink of insanity. Here, we see how the heightened prowess of our memory and the capacity to perceive matters from multiple perspectives highlight the razor-sharp edge that can cause profound wounds when mishandled.

Suffering changes us and it's a transformative process that can either rejuvenate or destroy. But what I find truly fascinating is how it has a way of chipping at our identity— fragmenting us. We become fragmented because of our unwillingness or inability to accept what is, so we create a sort of alter personality, one that's more suitable to face the inner hell we find ourselves in. Granted, some of these sub-identities will fight smaller disputes, but in the end, everyone will fragment at some point.

Suffering can certainly be quite a battle. Who, or what, will win? What parts of us will survive?

Furthermore, I perceive suffering much like the process of grieving—a natural response to hardships. While the journey of grief is unique for everyone, it's still marked by stages that are universally navigated. However, when accompanied by adequate, more importantly, empathetic support, one that reflects the wisdom in the Swedish proverb, "*Shared sorrow is half the sorrow. Shared joy is double joy*," individuals can transition through these stages more smoothly. This collective sharing[4] minimizes the risk of getting stuck in one phase, facilitating a somewhat seamless transition from one stage to the next until healing from the experience is attained.

> 4. Having positive and close relationships with others is considered among the top predictors of longevity.

If one cannot free oneself from their hell of prolonged suffering and continue to suffer without accepting and thus resisting, that is, when suffering has now become *complicated suffering*— a term I created and stems from the psychological concept of "complicated grief" which is used to describe a person that continues to grieve way past the average time it usually takes to process a loss.

Complicated suffering is apparent, other times it will be camouflaged by our personalities which makes it so that they can remain throughout a lifetime due to its insidious nature. Our bodies, however, unfailingly manifest signs when something is simply not right, potentially leading to severe illnesses despite our diligence in maintaining healthy lifestyle practices such as physical activity, nutritious eating, and proper sleep— our body always knows where we are psychologically.

An unresolved distress of the past will keep us locked to certain emotional triggers. Therefore, many of our emotional reactions to circumstances aren't solely about the circumstances at hand, instead, they will often stem from unresolved issues from our past. When we're "triggered," it feels like we're being reminded of something we've tried to bury, and we may even seek out relationships with people whose emotional sensitivities align with ours to avoid reopening those past wounds.

Often, we are so desperate to deliver ourselves from the complicated suffering that we will resort to maladaptive methods that will give us that jolt of pleasure even if it comes at the expense of our health down the road— as if to become the master of our emotions were a privilege we somehow missed out on.

Depression, anxiety, or anger appear to be the most common reactions to lingering suffering. The common thread underlying these reactions could be rooted in the concept of _control_. Depression seems to immerse individuals in the tragic aspects of circumstances, fostering feelings of despondency and lack of motivation due to a pervasive sense of powerlessness.

[Important side note: Many individuals find themselves perplexed when observing others who remain ensnared in depressive and unproductive states, which offer no apparent benefit to the individual and may eventually elicit feelings of apathy from observers. Common sentiments expressed include *"They are there because they want to be there"* or *"I don't understand why they don't get out"*. However, an aspect that often goes unacknowledged, yet can significantly contribute to this phenomenon, is what psychologists have termed as "learned helplessness". Learned helplessness, in psychiatry, has been defined as "*a condition in which a person has a sense of powerlessness, arising from a traumatic event or persistent failure to succeed*". They, more than likely, do not want to be in their situation; however, they do not see a way out, or worse yet... that's all they know. This concept could significantly contribute to understanding why individuals continue to be trapped in unfavorable circumstances.]

Anxiety occurs due to fear of the *potential* dangers that may or may not happen in the future—the fear of the unknown— however, *"no amount of anxiety will change what is bound to happen"* (source unidentified). Anger, on the other hand, can serve as a potent force that empowers individuals, allowing them to reclaim that feeling of personal agency that may have been previously taken away. Therefore, it makes sense to resort to anger as a coping mechanism but in the end, let's face it...neither is freeing. If nothing is done about it, all these reactions can become vicious cycles where we become depressed because we're depressed or anxious because we are anxious.

[Side note: There is no judgment here. Healing takes time, and everyone's journey in processing painful experiences is deeply personal.]

Additionally, fixation on the story (or trauma), occurs in the absence of a positive resolution. A positive resolution doesn't necessarily require an external remedy; it can also manifest internally through the creation of an *updated* mental map of past experiences, reflecting on or acknowledging them with newfound knowledge and wisdom. This approach proved to be incredibly valuable for me, a method I picked up thanks to Jordan B. Peterson, whom I've been an avid follower of since I was 27 years old, considering him an additional father figure. Dr. Peterson emphasizes that any traumatic experience older than 18 months which continues to negatively affect an individual, he suggests that the person is dwelling in the past because we did not *"map the territory well enough"* and our nervous system, usually felt in the form of anxiety, continues to send alarm signals attempting to tell us: *"There's holes in the way that you're looking at the world, and you've fallen in them once, and you don't know where they are, and you don't know how to fill them or how to walk around them. So, you can't forget them, you can't forget them, you can't forget them…"*, this can keep people chronically trapped in fight or flight. A significant part of me was stuck in past traumas for far too many years, unable to move past them. Carrying out this process of "mapping out," which I perceived as a form of *self-re-parenting*, involved treating myself as if I were a child in need of assistance, viewing it all from a third-person perspective.

It's worth noting that this was a gradual journey that spanned years and included numerous mental rehearsals. Moreover, I've integrated this technique with insights from Eastern philosophies, which proved to be quite compatible with my personal growth and healing journey.

In any case… moving on to another aspect that I've noticed and found very intriguing, is that humans have this deep need for "closure" which could be tied to human's innate attraction to symmetry. Symmetry is not limited to the visual; it can also be *perceived* through a sense of *balance* (this is important). Whether the mind naturally gravitates towards recognizing symmetry or if symmetry inherently exists is a contemplation that calls for reflections on the true nature of reality and a topic for another day. Regardless of which one is closer to the truth, symmetry holds significant value in many aspects of life. When a matter of personal significance feels "off" the natural inclination is to pursue solutions until the discrepancy is rectified, leading to a perceived successful resolution marked usually by what we call justice, fairness, or…*equilibrium.* And we are not usually satisfied until this is achieved, so in the meantime we are in a way disconnected or partially dead to what is right in front of us in the present moment because we have this deep need to resolve this imbalance that constantly nags and prevents us from enjoying what we currently have to the full extent. We do not sincerely appreciate what we hold because our minds are constantly shifting back and forth between the past and the future, hardly spending much, if any, time in the only place we truly ever have, which is the present moment.

Dutch philosopher, Baruch Spinoza, held the view that expanding our understanding of the causal structure of the world would not only lead to the comprehension of many "whys" but would also diminish its emotional grip on humans that can lead to suffering – this can be accomplished through various means. One approach is to acquire knowledge by reading works from great thinkers, while another method involves keen investigations both externally and internally. This should allow individuals to become less susceptible to the impact of their circumstances, ultimately attaining a state of equanimity. I'll share a brief portion of something I wrote in 2022 that can be related to this topic:

"My dad recently passed away, and if I could have known for a fact that he was smiling in some blissful Utopia, I'm quite certain my grief would have been greatly

reduced because having that information would make it more tolerable that he was no longer around. However, what if he wasn't in paradise? How could someone ever recover if they happened to know that their loved ones were in hell?

All I can think of at this moment is how grateful I am not to be given access to that information. The feeling of hope is working in the background, serving as armor, protecting me against potential hurtful truths... Not knowing can bring us more tranquility than knowing could ever bring, which is why the quote "ignorance is bliss" is so famous..."

In the case just presented there's a chance the information we receive may not be the one we hoped to receive. Thus, there's a cost associated with acquiring knowledge, yet there is also a price to pay when we opt for the easier path by remaining naive—pick your pain wisely. It becomes especially significant when we confront information that is both crucial and profoundly painful, disrupting the blissful ignorance we once cherished. However, staying within a comfort zone may offer a sense of security but it fails to provide us any real safety because there will always exist vital information that can only be found beyond our comfort zone, and this knowledge can significantly benefit us in ways we may not currently comprehend and perhaps never will comprehend if we continuously cling to outdated information within our safety bubble.

[Side note: At times, confronting difficulties becomes inevitable, so it's best to master the art of resolving them conclusively rather than attempting a mediocre solution that may resurface later—after all, a well-tied knot rarely needs retying.]

When discussing knowledge, I hold the belief that there is no such thing as acquiring knowledge prematurely. Even if comprehension doesn't immediately follow the need to put it into practice, it still sows a seed that may prove valuable in the future. Consider encountering a wise message in a book or quote that doesn't immediately resonate with you but, nevertheless, sounds nice. Years later, faced with adversity, that same message resurfaces with newfound clarity, triggering an "*Aha!*" moment. This delayed understanding often leads to a meaningful epiphany or sense of enlightenment, with the common thought of: "*Now I get it*". Here's a thought-provoking proposition to consider: Is it possible that we've all been subtly *prepared* to face challenges we have faced by the countless seeds of knowledge that have been quietly planted in our subconscious throughout our lives?... By the countless one-liners that at first just sounded good and got secretly stored in our subconscious, then later became our greatest source of clarity during hardships allowing us to navigate these with much more ease? Of course, there's no way to tell but it's still interesting to ponder about.

Another aspect to consider is how we attribute subjective significance to everything we experience, imbuing it with our own *meaning*, much like how we assign our interpretation to an abstract painting or an inkblot test in a psychoanalytic session. The assigned significance we place on our experiences (or people) is what gives rise to our diverse reactions. While I place no complaint over this natural tendency precisely because it is natural, it's still crucial to recognize that the interpretations, significance, or meaning, we attach to aspects of our lives are often influenced by external sources. How many of these inherited interpretations—infused with someone else's subjective meaning— do we apply to our realities, whether consciously or subconsciously? But more importantly, now that we've adopted many of these…how *accurate* were these meaningful interpretations made by its initial evaluator? And are these still relevant, or are we clinging to antiquated notions of truth that have become obsolete in the contemporary context?

Furthermore, those who have imparted their knowledge to us also confront the obstacle of language. Will they utilize this medium effectively? Can they convey their profound insights to us without diluting their valuable wisdom? That's if it was indeed close to some higher truth [most accurate]. Well, it depends on what *they* believed to be accurate at the time…this is yet another discussion for another day.

We can only hope that those who have conveyed these meanings to us have provided at least a *somewhat* accurate interpretation. Or that its falsehood unveils a hidden truth just like there's a bit of truth inside every joke. We must acknowledge that achieving absolute certainty when it comes to the *validity of meaning* will be challenging, since interpretations frequently, if not always, entail subjective elements— after all… we are living in a subjective reality even if we attempt to make it objective every opportunity we get. Nevertheless, everyone retains the right to attribute whatever meaning they choose to the aspects of their reality. All I will suggest is: aim to reach a point where outdated information no longer traps you in perpetual irrationality.

As I mentioned previously, wise are those who maintain a perpetual intellectual humility, remaining open to incoming information for the enhancement of a more precise comprehension of reality. This work always starts within. Start by delving into your depths, understanding yourself better, and scrutinizing the validity of your self-assessments with brutal honesty. Question your pain and suffering, question their lengths and severity. You might resist doing this, and you also might do it quite badly at the beginning but continue to practice this anyway. It's crucial to challenge yourself *sincerely* during this process. Witness in a non-judgmental manner to whatever may arise as you seek explanations for internal phenomena, be it a personality trait, a thought, a memory, or an emotion because if you attempt to dig with high judgment, then you stand a high chance that your persona might not show you all that there is to see due to the fear of being harshly judged and not to mention the potential for changes, since we know we have a tendency to resist change.

By becoming your own experimental subject, and mastering the art of introspection with honesty and intense concentration, you will progressively cultivate understanding, empathy, and ultimately, compassion for both yourself and others. Over time, you'll shed mental distortions that might have otherwise caused unnecessary difficulties or distress. Even if a few of these distortions manage to evade detection, resulting in occasional missteps—something entirely human— the ability to introspect remains a valuable tool, offering a path towards equanimity during challenges, provided we're willing to engage with sincerity in the process.

In brief:

The way I see it, suffering is a process. It is a journey that leads to a refined outcome. Without undergoing the rigors of suffering, achieving this sort of refinement would be nearly impossible. Certainly, individuals can still develop and mature without enduring profound hardships, yet they may miss out on cultivating fortitude, adaptability, and compassion that comes exclusively from undergoing suffering – provided they can successfully navigate their inner struggles and derive such virtues, rather than succumbing to heightened levels of neuroticism, bitterness, and/or nihilism.

There is an additional skill, a very precious one, that develops also with suffering which is the wisdom to know which battle needs fighting and which one does not, in more romantic words, the wisdom to recognize when we should put our sword and armor down. Therefore, suffering provides us with special insights into aspects of life and ourselves that happiness cannot reveal…how else would we uncover the depths of our strength if were never given the chance to truly test its limits?

Also, we are beings with much to learn and this calls for the continual falling on our faces. The only person that does not fall is the person who knows it all, and such a person does not exist. However, do not allow things to break you indefinitely— attempt to stand above it. Over time, either the stumbles will decrease, or you'll find humor in them. In both scenarios, you'll have garnered wisdom, perspective, and lessons learned, making the experience beneficial to you no matter what.

"Beyond the mountains, are more mountains."

–Haitian proverb.

Chapter II. Cornered by Life

Maybe this hasn't happened to everyone, but for those who have had at least one experience where they felt compelled to make a decision without any worthy alternatives, it can certainly make them feel anxious and frustrated as if life has unfairly or unjustly cornered them. While they ponder on the few options that might exist, an internal voice warns against those choices, like an instinct to hold off and wait a little longer— but the waiting game has not been one of our stronger suits and neither has been learning to listen to the guidance of our intuition. Undergoing such a situation can be profoundly challenging, particularly when it entails sacrificing one's aspirations in favor of serving others. What adds to the difficulty of this situation is the *uncertainty* of ever being able to reclaim the chance to fulfill those aspirations later— the envisioned self, shaped by those accomplishments is out of reach. While this could just be temporary, it can certainly feel like a permanent defeat.

I've observed individuals who navigated and adapted to this situation with admirable ease. In contrast, my journey has been a tale of persistent struggle and quite frankly, a narrative that persists to this day… though fortunately, not as much.

    One particular morning, with my cup of coffee as my only company, I sat immersed in thought where much like smoke that suddenly materializes and delicately floats through the air, so did my recollections over the last few weeks and so I began to contemplate on these. I should add that I had been feeling frustrated, short-tempered, and overall irritated, this was fueled by a sense of immobility—I felt cornered. Inherent in my nature has been my drive but coupled with my track record for impatience makes sustained stillness quite the challenge for me. Since I was not able to find any obvious external solutions, I felt no other option but to go searching for it internally. The process involved eliminating numerous thoughts and emotions that I, at first, deemed "crucial" but were in fact interfering with the actual solution or answer I was seeking.

    During this, I decided to journal what was within, to just simply write and observe what emerged. Documenting our feelings and thoughts in this way can provide a clearer map into our inner world allowing for a more productive examination than if they remain within where they stand the risk of becoming tangled with countless passing thoughts, emotions, or ideas making it harder to decode. By jotting them down, we can extract some of these for closer examination, free from the weight of their internal entanglement.

"So here I am, sitting, contemplating on the word: "deserve". The reason I began to think about this word is because I was pretty sure that was at the core of what was making me irritable and bitter in the situation I found myself in.

"I deserve better", the classic thought. Upon deeper reflection on the matter, I got a sense of threat…
What If I stop seeking what my being perceives as "better" or worthy of deserving? What does that mean for me? What would my future look like?

As I paid close attention to these internal questions, an uneasy feeling began to emerge. This would mean I would be letting go entirely of any ambition, or vision I had where I saw myself being happy and fulfilled— even knowing very well these two states do not last, but for some reason I, like others, continue to pursue satisfaction or happiness, being fully aware that it usually is not everlasting once attained.

Our mind restlessly yearning for the next best thing.

Then I began to create a sort of buffer between myself and the thoughts and feelings.

"Surrendering" ... Why does that word cause me such alarm? I wondered. Perhaps the reason for this alarm could be because my being realizes this requires a psychological death; an ego death... To relinquish a mental model of what I considered "ideal".

So many more thoughts and emotions began to appear. The primary ones were fear and worry about what others would think of me if I stopped pursuing what I considered to be "what I deserve" because those goals happened to be aligned with what society would consider "a somebody"; admirable, impressive, respected, and therefore, valuable. Afraid of the societal implications of lacking those wonderful labels and instead being seen as less valuable, ordinary, weak, and non-important.

Soon, I began to think about the countless people who exist on this planet that have also been cornered by life, so to speak, but in more permanent ways. People who most of us would consider a "nobody" yet have such a good spirit and hold an optimistic outlook on life versus being bitter and resentful for the cards they were dealt. For instance, how many people live in unimaginable impoverished conditions and still manage to remain generous? How many people have lost their eyesight, and their enthusiasm remains intact? How many have lost a child and continue to be loving towards life and God?

They have so much to teach me... These people perhaps do not realize it, but they carry a sort of toughness that can never be obtained by any "I-deserve-better" mentality. They are beyond that. It's as if deep down they have an innate knowing that has allowed them to not take themselves, or life's curveballs, so seriously. They tread lightly."

After I penned those thoughts down, I felt ashamed of my attitude towards life at that moment. In a world where our self-judgment holds such substantial weight due to its degree of brutality pretty much makes the need for divine scrutiny unnecessary. And should our self-judgment falter, the world around us is quick to offer its ample supply.

In any case, one should at least attempt not to be so harsh on oneself for regressing into our common human tendencies of entitlement and ungratefulness.

"Shower upon him every earthly blessing, drown him in a sea of happiness, so that nothing but bubbles of bliss can be seen on the surface; give him economic prosperity, such that he should have nothing else to do but sleep, eat cakes and busy himself with the continuation of his species, and even then out of sheer ingratitude, sheer spite, man would play you some nasty trick. He would even risk his cakes and would deliberately desire the most fatal rubbish, the most uneconomical absurdity, simply to introduce into all this positive good sense his fatal fantastic element. It is just his fantastic dreams, his vulgar folly that he will desire to retain, simply in order to prove to himself – as though that were so necessary – that men still are men and not the keys of a piano, which the laws of nature threaten to control so completely... And that is not all: even if man really were nothing but a piano-key, even if this were proved to him by natural science and mathematics, even then he would not become reasonable, but would purposely do something perverse out of simple ingratitude, simply to gain his point."

– Notes From Underground, Fyodor Dostoevsky

I believe the ultimate path to breaking free from the feeling of being *cornered* lies in freeing oneself from oneself – battling the mind against mind. Since, in the end, we are the only ones that place our own constraints. However, the challenge extends beyond that. It's about accomplishing this without shutting down our hearts, and *sincerely* learning to like what we don't like, appreciating it for what it is and *as it is*. Of course, this endeavor is one of those that's easier said than done. It can be extraordinarily difficult and quite painful. Its significance is not solely attributed to the degree of immense challenge but also to the profound nature of such a journey –the battle with oneself as the ultimate confrontation. Because of this, it stands as a loftier pursuit, transcending the mere accumulation of accolades, prestige, or wealth.

You'll find yourself lingering in this metaphorical corner until you've fulfilled what is being asked of you. It's really up to each of us how long we stay there— more often than not, it's a mental thing, meaning… we can change our circumstances based on the perspective we wish to see it as. And this will depend on which level of reality we usually live in. *What do I mean by this?* I'll explain more in Part II. Here is when we must recognize the potential call to relinquish denial—the very denial that may have been causing our anxiety, anger, or depression— and where acceptance can start to take root. Therefore, being cornered by life serves as a necessary checkmate.

Furthermore, we have this tendency that when we have an obstacle that obstructs our path in a certain direction, we immediately chase after it to correct it. According to our history, *the chase* has been a long-held human habit since that's where the thrill is. One compelling explanation for this can be found in the psychological term known as: *hedonic adaptation.* Its meaning is straightforward, it describes how we acclimate to life's pleasures, privileges, blessings, or whichever way you wish to label it, such as our partner, home, income, career, etc… and because we can become accustomed to these, they eventually lose their allure, leaving us persistently yearning for more or better; we develop as sort of addiction to the feeling we get while we are *chasing* or the feeling we get right after we have attained X,Y,Z, yet this ecstasy doesn't last very long, except in the cases of relationships with the prime example of the "honey-moon phase" which can sometimes last up to two years. Nevertheless, the initial excitement and rush always dissipates.

The problem is not striving for advancement since I have always been one to advocate for ongoing improvements. The issue arises when the pursuit takes the best of us, especially when our efforts fail to yield the results we wanted. *Does the inability to achieve signify that we'll never succeed?* Not necessarily, but in the meantime, the absence of attainment surely can be maddening, triggering a range of negative emotions that not only impact us but also those closest to us.

Now, certain scenarios, such as instances involving psychological or physical abuse, are undeniably detrimental and require a transition to a healthier, "better" environment for the individual to thrive. *But what if someone finds themselves trapped (cornered) by life in such dire circumstances? What then?* This is a grave issue that demands sensitivity. If, indeed, there seems to be no way out, then the only path left may be to delve inward. I'll elaborate further on this in part II, as it entails a significant shift in perspective, requiring an entirely different frame of reference. However, I must emphasize that even this situation [the abuse] isn't impermanent. What's permanent is impermanence itself. I can wish thousands of times for this to never be the case for anyone, and cry myself to sleep every night for those that have or currently are experiencing this, however, there will always (though I hope not forever) be individuals at various stages of their personal evolution who inflict pain and suffering upon others in unimaginably cruel ways. Thinking how such heartbreaking instances are happening at this very moment can certainly bring us back down, placing our feet on the ground once again with humility— one must never forget those who are suffering and have no one to save them or speak for them. I am speaking for them and acknowledging them now and dedicate this part, though brief, in their honor.

In less tragic or extreme circumstances, our perception of what is "better" is tied to our current perspectives and identity— or the perspectives we have adopted by others based on what they considered to be "better" or "superior"– and we formulate mechanisms or methods that will help us get our desires met, the faster the better, which is a key hype of modern technology.

Nevertheless, I shall reiterate that fortunate is the one who, when confronted with a sense of being stuck, can awaken to the realization that it presents an important opportunity to reevaluate what has been overlooked or deflected. Otherwise, we will repeatedly encounter very similar situations that will persist in making us feel stuck (or cornered) in the same negative patterns. For example, when we notice a recurring theme in our lives where we'll consistently say, *"I keep bumping into the same problem of...".* And just as I suggested in the earlier chapter on pain and suffering, the same applies here; this is a time for *honest* introspection otherwise we are doomed to trip over the same rock. One of the things I had to admit while I was in "my corner" was coming to the brutal realization that I was imitating actions I had condemned in others. It took a lot of honesty on my part to recognize this cycle and once I saw it, there was no way I could not see it and felt like a complete hypocrite whenever I fell back to these old ways, knowing very well they were unfair. My being would cringe each time I ignored it out of mere selfishness.

Now, for others, it can be a time for gathering lost humility and re-learning to appreciate even the smallest things in our lives we have taken for granted, not succumbing to the cognitive tendency presented by "hedonic adaptation"— this was something I also had to work on while in "my corner". In fact, it might be quite impossible to make any wholesome and sincere changes without the key ingredients of humility and gratitude.

[Side note: I realize I use "humility" an awful lot, but I truly believe that it is our greatest weapon.]

I will conclude this chapter with a passage from a phenomenal book I've read that was published solely for the inmates at the California San Quentin penitentiary 1970s, titled 'Inside Out'. This passage was written by one of the inmates at this prison who was sent to solitary confinement (talk about being cornered or stuck). I should also mention that this person had previous experience with long sessions of meditation lasting up to an hour, which came especially useful to him when in solitary:

"I could understand why even firm and well-developed intellects break down in such a state of confinement and readily turn towards insanity." ... "But for those unaccustomed it is not easy to control and steady the mind pulled in a thousand directions." ... "In the hope of mental solace and resting the overheated brain I looked at the beauties of nature outside, but with that solitary tree, a sliced sky and the cheerless prospects in the prison how long can the mind, in such a state, find consolation? I looked towards the black wall. Gazing at the lifeless white surface the mind seemed to grow even more hopeless,

releasing the agony of the imprisoned condition the brain was restless in the cage." … "I looked around, at last found some large black ants moving about a hole in the ground, and I spent some time watching their efforts and movements. Later I noticed some tiny red ants. Soon there was a big battle between the back and the red, the black ants began to bite and kill the ants. I felt an intense charity and sympathy for those unjustly treated red ants and tried to save them from the black killers. This gave me occupation and something to think about. Thanks to the ants I passed a few days like this." – Inside Out, 1976.

Chapter III. Wants vs Needs

"I searched where I least wanted to search.

In the depths of my mind- in the darkness.

There were many unknown faces waiting.

Then one by one, they began to scream horribly at me.

Attempting with all their might to scare me.

As one face appeared and screamed, another would suddenly appear and take over.

Then another, and another…

Faces overlapping, shifting, and fleeing rapidly.

Their screams growing louder as they lingered.

They sought to inflict suffering to drive me away.

Despite my fear, my presence remained.

Finally, I began to scream back at them.

Screams fueled by the lost times I could not scream.

They dispersed and gradually vanished into the void.

Suddenly, emerging from a dense fog, appeared an old tree with a single blackbird perched on one of its branches. As I walked closer towards the tree, I intuitively knew the bird had been anticipating my arrival, and patiently waiting as I drew near. This bird had a message for me because it knew I had questions. The black bird said:

"Hell is below and Heaven above. All you can do is go right or left and walk in between them."

After that, my head moved to look around and behind the tree to examine what sort of path lay ahead. The tree and the bird slowly disappeared, leaving only the lingering fog and the road ahead. I continued my journey.

The journey led me to a blazing desert with scorching winds and swirling sands relentlessly blowing hectically towards me, hindering my sight and unable to see more than a few steps ahead — I felt suffocating nervousness.

The blackbird returned to my aid. I sensed the gentle prickle of its claws on my skin as it lifted me away from the sandstorm inferno. The bird traveled with such speed that time seemed to become visible and unfold before my eyes resembling red satin sheets—the softest and most mesmerizing sheets I had ever witnessed.

It brings me to the doorstep of an old and abandoned castle, then flies away without providing any form of guidance or instructions.

Driven by curiosity, I pushed the castle door open. I cautiously walk in.

I quickly observed that the interior was entirely vacant, yet it was peculiar in the sense that it was so empty that not even a trace of dust had accumulated. It was impeccably pristine.

"How interesting", I thought.

The space was enveloped in darkness, with the exception of the foyer which was illuminated by a solitary light. There was something distinctive about this light—it evoked a sense of reverence.

Simultaneously, I took note of the elegant black and white checkered floor. Shortly after observing the checkered floor, I became aware of a singular chess piece standing at the center of this potential playing field, precisely positioned beneath the light. The chess piece towering over me with great height.

I recognized this as a move that had been played— a strategy implemented.

What remains unknown to me is what precise piece was in the middle of the floor or what move it represented."[1]

1. Written by me in April 2023. The essence of this vision I had is imbued with uncertainty, reflecting a deep longing to progress in a specific direction. However, this direction awaits guidance from me, which requires a clear understanding of my genuine desires— "What do you want?".

Every living organism has non-negotiable needs that must be met to continue to live. On the other hand, we have *desires*, an aspect not shared by all living organisms.

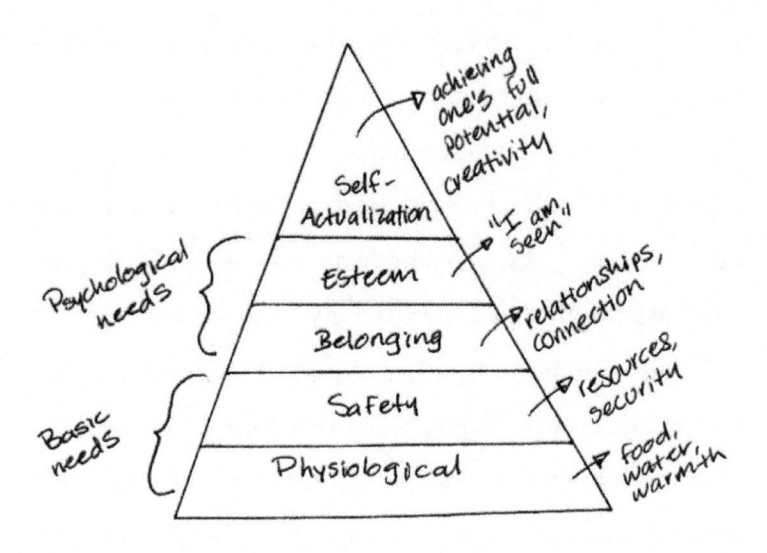

Maslow's hierarchy of needs is a widely recognized framework that outlines human's various needs. We can agree that the foundational layer—comprising essentials like food, water, and warmth—is crucial for maintaining the optimal functioning of our brain and body throughout the day and thus life.

According to Maslow, once our physiological needs are met, then and only then, are we receptive enough to either seek or receive our psychological/emotional needs. But quite frankly, I find this hierarchy questionable. Consider the question of whether one can summon sufficient motivation to pursue vital resources for survival without meaningful relationships to live for?

Therefore, I believe these [physiological resources] to be necessary though not sufficient…For instance, if I were the sole inhabitant of this world, my needs and/or wants would not be the same ones as the ones I have today and even though this is a simple and obvious fact, it is far from basic. In this case, perhaps my being would eventually find it meaningless to pursue food, water, and/or warmth since I would have a deep longing for companionship and connection with another being to fulfill the need of being "seen" – in other words, we need others to witness our existence and us theirs. Therefore, it's crucial to recognize that Maslow's hierarchy of needs works because it assumes that we have other humans to stay alive for. In this case, it makes sense that one must attend to their physiological needs before the pursuit of other needs.

However, if we look at it in circular reasoning, we won't naturally seek to fulfill our physiological needs unless we have something meaningful to live for such as relationships with others. Conversely, we also won't find that meaningful purpose in life unless our psychological needs are satisfied.

It seems impossible to separate them [physiological and psychological needs]. This interdependence stands as another example that mirrors the inseparability of yin and yang, good and evil, up and down, black and white. Moreover, trying to establish a sequential order, such as arguing that yin comes before yang or vice versa, may overlook the inherent nature of their coexistence, a concept that could also apply to humans and their hierarchy of needs. I realize this might be quite a bold idea, but it's still just an idea—a funny thought. Can we be so sure that the order represented by Maslow's hierarchy is an absolute truth for anyone regardless of their circumstances? It's worth considering that while the hierarchy provides a useful framework for understanding human motivation, it's important to recognize that individuals may navigate these needs more fluidly and dynamically, sometimes addressing higher-level needs before lower-level ones, depending on their unique circumstances and psychological makeup, but again, this is just a thought…

 Something else that came to mind, one I found intriguing when contemplating on "witnessing the existence of others" was: as observers, it appears to boil down to witnessing the interactions and reactions among atoms as they engage in the process of forming molecules –through the construction or dissolution of bonds—giving shape to the world around us. I realize this sidetracks a bit, but I could not bring myself to remove it because it somehow connects in my mind and my mind found this relevant to the topic still. In the least of cases, it can provide a mere and brief amusement that deviates from the seriousness we are often trained to adhere to.

Delving back into wants versus needs…

As we progress through various stages of development, from infancy to late adulthood, our fundamental physiological needs remain constant in essence, yet the quantities require an increase. For instance, the demand for water and food grows as we age compared to our infantile requirements. Even individuals who undertake fasting periods must eventually consume sufficient food and water to meet the basic cellular needs necessary for maintaining their adult-size bodies. Achieving this necessitates providing the body with substantially more sustenance than an infant or toddler would consume—which would explain the biological reason why we progressively ask for more, or at least where it all began. This trend also applies to psychological/emotional needs but places quite a significant role on the people we meet in this life because if you think about it, they are responsible for providing us the emotional safety, connection, and recognition we "need". Following Maslow's hierarchy of needs, we can only reach our "*full potential*" once our basic physiological and psychological needs are fulfilled by these external sources. So, no pressure, folks...

In terms of wants/desires, these will also match our current stage of development but now these will reflect an additional layer which is the aspect of our culture, heritage, and/or the society we live in, thus, wants/desires become more varied and complex, and not as straightforward as our physiological needs tend to be.

Both, needs and wants, seem to provide us with different types of satisfaction. A need gives us what is necessary for fulfilling what is most vital to sustain life, yet it doesn't necessarily equate to profound pleasure. Whereas a "want" or a "desire" tends to be of an entirely different nature, one that seeks actual pleasure or joy. Consider, for instance, that we survived on a simple diet consisting of only beans and rice, which lacks the sensory satisfaction of a more flavorful meal like a pizza would. In this context, pizza symbolizes a want or desire; it meets our nutritional needs while also satisfying a craving for pleasure due to its flavorful combination, releasing higher levels of dopamine (and other neurotransmitters) compared to meeting only our basic nutritional needs. Nevertheless, it can be tricky at times to differentiate a *want* versus a *need* which is why it's common to hear these two words being used interchangeably. But if we are honest, we can detect the times when what was once considered a "need" was perhaps a craving. *A craving for what?* Is there such a thing as an empty craving? Could it be connected to an unrecognized need, causing us to feel depleted and thus resulting in cravings? If this is the case, could we ever deem a want as "bad"?

When we cannot attain a particular desire/want, we tend to seek alternative means to fulfill these, sometimes going to great lengths. We've devised ingenious methods to satisfy desires if our initial ones are unattainable for any reason. Therefore, we consistently possess a secondary desire ready to step in as a backup. Maybe Freud's notion of the "pleasure principle" holds some truth, as it suggests that we are perpetually in pursuit of gratifying moments, or dopamine rushes. This could explain why we often find it challenging to put a stop to overindulgence even if it can have detrimental consequences in the long term. Nevertheless, I remain vigilant on the idea that perhaps this inclination originates from a deeper sense of emptiness, an ongoing "void" that intensifies as individuals become increasingly absorbed in what society perceives as "success" but in reality, leads to a life enslaved by work rigid schedules, monotonous routines, and overall, poor quality of life.

So, what should one do about this dilemma? What would happen if we simply gave in to our every whim, given that these were hypothetically rooted in an unmet need? Some might think that the world would become completely chaotic, and to prevent this we set guidelines, ethics, laws, and rules, because humans need help *controlling* their impulses. This is fair. I guess the problem has more to do with *quantity* rather than quality. However, I find it puzzling because society enforces ethics and moral conduct, shames or punishes those that go astray, yet flaunts and gives easy access to empty desires that not only are highly attractive and enticing but dangerously addictive to humans.

Nevertheless, as Fyodor Dostoevsky said in his book '*Notes from Underground*' (passage previously shared in chapter II); "*Shower upon him every earthly blessing*" … "*He would even risk his cakes and would deliberately desire the most fatal rubbish*" … simply to prove that we are not "*piano keys*".

I find that it's not solely our desires that can inflict us pain, but even our fundamental needs can also have similar effects since we can also, and have, blamed our suffering on our "needs" for yielding only the bare minimum. On the other hand, we blame our "wants" for causing the relentless pursuit of something better, perpetually seeking the proverbial greener grass on the other side— keeping up with the Joneses— taking up all of our efforts, draining our energy, or demoralizing us, only to keep finding ourselves continually coming back for more, reaching for that dangling carrot we will never have.

The wisdom in the East shares something worth keeping in mind when it comes to our desires. The Buddhist Four Noble Truths[2] warn us about the danger of our desires as sources for great suffering. Many will assume that the answer then is to repress such desires; not quite… All Buddhism suggests is not to allow ourselves to be *ruled* by our desires. Or as great theologian, Alan Watts puts it "…*doesn't mean you lose your appetite for dinner. It means that you stop grabbing*".

2. Four Noble Truths, briefly state (i) life is suffering, (ii) what causes more suffering such as cravings and lack of understanding, (iii) ending suffering through awakening, (iv) the path to end suffering.

Here's another thought. Given the amount of time and effort humans have remained on this dynamic— constantly looking for more and better—is at all possible that we have within us most of what we could ever possibly need, and can fulfill us in such meaningful ways that we simply cannot fathom since we have never been taught how to access this? Of course, this applies once we have reached a certain age of maturity, since this would not be possible in the early stages of development, or it at the very least would pose a great unnecessary degree of risk to children, especially infants.

As adults, why is it so difficult to access this within us? If it were meant to be accessed on our own, wouldn't it be more straightforward? Some may even find it illogical and argue that if it presents such difficulties, it therefore must mean that it goes against our natural inclinations. However, our own experiences have proven to contradict this idea, as we often engage in harmful behaviors or thought cycles that lead to intensified feelings of anxiety, sadness, jealousy, anger, or despair. At times, we may even become severely anxious about situations that are entirely creations of our imagination and have not actually occurred as if our being momentarily struggles to differentiate between what is real and what is not real. How is this behavior logical or straightforward? Or could we truly say this is our *natural* inclination—to be constantly on the brink of psychosis? We truly are quite strange. Why do we insist on complicating the simplicity that life can provide?

Part Two
Standing Back

Soft Warning

I must admit, writing this book turned out to be more challenging than I anticipated, but composing the second part proved to be even more difficult since it required articulating observations about existence in simple terms on aspects that are quite ineffable or, at the very least, difficult to express in a manner that others can fully comprehend unless they have also glimpsed at what I am attempting to convey. As a result, certain sections may appear more complex to grasp than others, trust me, I hardly understand it myself. However, do not let it dissuade you from continuing.

"If you're going through hell, keep going" – Winston Churchill

Chapter IV. Freedom of Choice

We all inherently yearn for control over our lives—it's natural. None of us relishes the feeling of being trapped, devoid of alternatives, and compelled to accept a predetermined fate. We crave the autonomy to make our own choices often (maybe not so often for others) resisting the imposition of decisions by either external forces or individuals. Consider this thought: if we were to cede control and let others decide for us, there's a significant chance of them making mistakes because they may not understand or be aware of our true or hidden desires and/or needs. This is why most people prefer to make their own decisions—to minimize the risk of errors. Even if we make mistakes, at least we can take ownership of them, which may provide a sense of security or pride. *But what should be made of the occasions when we do blame others or external factors for our own errors?*

Alternatively: what if *life* were to make such decisions on our behalf? Would we dare claim that our judgment to make decisions for ourselves is far superior and closer to precision compared to *life*, or nature, itself? This question gives pause for a second thought, doesn't it?

After all, we're discussing something beyond our immediate understanding of the universe and our relevance to it.

These sorts of questions prompt one to reflect on the enduring enigma of free will. I've spent considerable time wrestling with this idea and its opposing perspectives, pondering whether we have control over our actions or if every aspect of our lives is indeed determined. Of course, there's no way to ever know the answer to this question, yet it can still be an uncomfortable proposition for many to consider; how perhaps our freedom to choose has always been but an illusion. I'm not affirming this notion either; I'm simply expressing thoughts without reaching a conclusion, because how could anyone ever know for certain? We can't. Here is where one must decide for oneself based on what one believes works for them at the time. Also –and this is quite important— no one is obliged to maintain the same beliefs indefinitely. Actually…I hope most people can traverse different beliefs to see what else is out there, try them all out—why not? Let them cross your mind for a moment, consider them, consider them all. The act of considering doesn't necessarily require you to make any major decisions based on them, it just means you're checking them out from afar and see what sorts of thoughts or feelings they elicit, and based on whatever thoughts and feelings do emerge then I would say, question these and consult where they might be coming from and why they are there. You would be surprised how many of our beliefs have been implanted subtly without our awareness and how many of these might have no real basis other than for the reason of: *"it's what I've been taught"*.

Going back to the contemplation on making decisions— can we truly separate the decisions we make or even the decisions others have made on our behalf, from the influence of life's, or nature's, intelligence? Is it possible that all decisions are intricately intertwined with its [life] subtle guidance by constantly nudging us in certain directions?

Moving on…

From a deterministic perspective, everything is constantly operating under the laws of nature such as cause and effect—a law we have all witnessed. If determinism holds true, then to what extent? Framed differently, how much of our existence is already determined, that is… pre-determined or pre-destined? This is what we often refer to as "fate", "destiny" or "fatalism". On the other hand, proponents of free will argue for its existence primarily due to considerations of moral responsibility; people need to be held accountable for their actions otherwise what justification would exist for punishment?

Based on what I've noticed, the more I scrutinize my past, the harder it becomes to claim that I've truly had the freedom to choose since these events have unfolded with such immaculate accuracy, down to the most minute details that I would often consider trivial or not even notice. It seems hard to fathom that I could orchestrate such perfect alignment with so many moving pieces, therefore something much greater than myself, given my virtuous limitations… must be the source responsible for this master plan. Right?

In Hinduism[1]—one of the, if not the, oldest organized religions in history—they believe in the idea of reincarnation as part of our life's cyclical process, where our soul does not die, only the body dies. However, I suspect that their idea of reincarnation goes much deeper than what we in the West tend to think of when we hear the word "reincarnation" which is commonly taken as inconceivable merely due to its degree of unfamiliarity. An additional belief that compliments the idea of reincarnation, also part of the Hindu religion, is that since they also believe in the illusion of "the self"; that is, the individual as a separate entity from a greater source, it makes every new life that enters the world a sort of proof of reincarnation— an idea also proposed by Alan Watts, who spent his life studying various religions with immense diligence and passion. This would work since it's not based on the previous identity one once had, and is instead based on their inner *essence* and what it's connected to, if that makes sense? However, I'm not qualified to delve much deeper into this topic and can only speak of what I consider to be the most preliminary, or basic, aspects of it.

     Moving on... It is also believed [in Hinduism] that the consequences of our actions in this life will have a ripple effect and can even shape our future life, this is what they refer to as "karma", and every reincarnation is an opportunity for us to resolve this karmic debt by living in more moral ways each time— a belief that is also held by Buddhists and Taoists. Looking at it solely from a physics perspective, this embodies the principle of cause and effect in its purest form. The only difference is that there isn't a limitation, or boundary, placed on how far this law extends.

     In any case, I could not help but follow this thread of thoughts that led to wondering about the first infraction, or "sin" by humans that initiated this "karmic debt"— the religious event referred to as *the fall of man*. The Book of Genesis in the Bible recounts the moment of the fall of man when Adam and Eve disobeyed God by consuming the forbidden fruit from the tree of knowledge and this disobedience set in motion a cascade of consequences that have reverberated through the human race ever since.

Furthermore, in his insightful book 'Food of the Gods,' ethnobiologist Terence McKenna (another mind I highly value) suggests that the Tree of Knowledge could have symbolized psychedelic mushrooms or other naturally occurring psychedelic substances encountered by our ancient ancestors. He proposes that these substances played a crucial role in the unprecedented rapid expansion of human consciousness or cognition, marking a pivotal moment in our evolutionary journey.

I'm aware that delving into this topic will certainly raise many more questions ["whys"] and there's a risk of it being met with great skepticism, which is completely understandable. If you don't believe in karma or reincarnation, just pretend I didn't say any of it and move on. However, I do want to bring to our awareness that we must recognize that the "whys" will remain bottomless because therein lies our track-record for wanting to dissect things, seek meaning, and find answers, and this sometimes makes it so that we generate questions that only lead us into murkier waters.

Nonetheless, individuals can break free from the illusions and reignite long-forgotten insights into our true nature and what we might be doing here, arriving at a level of understanding regarding the most fundamental aspects of life or existence. Throughout history, we know of notable figures who have achieved this, such as Christ, Buddha, Laozi (Lao Tzu), Ramakrishna, Gandhi, Mandela, and others. These individuals exemplify a deep understanding that transcends mere knowledge; they no longer speak wisdom, they *wear wisdom*. Many of them have no interest in becoming involved with all the intricacies of theology or science and have also left behind most, if not all, questions since they realized there is no difference between the question and the questioner.

I could continue sharing documented remarks from more historically brilliant and wise souls who have shared their belief in reincarnation, fate, and/or karma. However, such evidence may seem less significant considering that opposing views have also been brought forth by other respected individuals and religions, essentially canceling out anything I've attempted to share and what some might regard as mere "wishful thinking"[1].

> 1. The spiritual journey isn't merely wishful thinking; rather, it stands as one of the most challenging paths due to its demand for learning to extend unconditional love and compassion to others.

Considering all of this, hopefully many can understand why it continues to be challenging for me to entirely reject the notion of free will, since it may exist in a more nuanced and complex manner, making it simultaneously present and absent. Despite our urge for a clear-cut response when it comes to the topic of free will, forcing ourselves into either extreme may be quite unproductive for a concept as elusive as this one and may instead require the consideration of both possibilities.

It's intriguing to note that regardless of whatever the case might be, we continue to think as if we *do* have the freedom to choose. This sense of agency is significant to acknowledge and could explain why we keep engaging in the act of making choices, but then again… there will be some individuals who instead exploit the concepts of determinism (no free will) or fatalism (fate) as a shield to evade personal responsibility.

Here's another question some might be wondering— I certainly did. *What would the point be in thinking we have free will if we were to suppose that everything is predetermined?* Of course, here we find ourselves facing yet another question with no definitive answer, but I'll still attempt to give it my best shot.

I would say that perhaps the reason why we hold the perception of the liberty to choose could be because it is what allows us to *reflect* on our lives. This is precisely why it was vital for the first sin (the fall of man) to occur, or early ancestors to ingest natural psychedelic substances thousands of years ago that accelerated our cognitive evolution sharpening our higher thinking faculty.

See… within every opportunity that's presented to us to make a choice, lie innumerable thoughts. These thoughts exist between, *or beyond*, the duality we are all familiar with. Before we go in one direction or another, say for instance, before we say "yes" or "no", this additional world –or layer of reality— makes itself known to us, and its curiously usually in the face of the unknown (before we make a decision). This realm brings forth thoughts that have not necessarily picked a side, per se, they are merely representing *what is,* or as we have come to label it:

"possibilities". As many possibilities our conscious awareness can recognize during this short period of time. However, due to our inherent tendency to pass judgments, our brains almost immediately, take these "possibilities" get mentally filtered, also at great speed, in order to organize them into mental categories; one denoted as "positive potential" and the other as "negative potential". This sorting out process is based on our cost-to-benefit ratio assessment, often stemming from what we've experienced in the past while considering what we would like to see happen in the future. But before we get to this point (deciding), there is a moment where we stood briefly –and I mean briefly— in the middle of *nowhere*; in that space beyond the duality, I previously mentioned. It's a different realm we don't usually spend too much time in because external forces constantly pressure us to make up our minds and pick a side; make an ultimate decision in one direction or another. There are hardly many instances where we can simply allow things to just *be*, without the need of placing a value on them as "good" or "bad". Looking at art could allow us to exercise this, but we've been wearing our "judge" hats for so long that it can be hard to even take this hat off when observing something as subjective as art.

I have a suspicion that in this space, this layer, or realm— though our visits are usually brief— contains so much more than we might think. It could be the source of immense potential of profound wisdom and compassion, but also a source of great fulfillment and completion, because it appears to appreciate everything *just as it is*, prior to being divided into "right" or "wrong". However, we usually only extract superficial insights from it to continue with our daily routines.

Moving on…

While we're reviewing as many of the *possibilities* as we can before placing a label on them, one of these possibilities might make eye contact with us even if it lasts a split second, but it *nudges our curiosity* which triggers further inquiry. Now, if we did not hold the perception that we had the freedom to choose, then perhaps we wouldn't delve into these introspective investigations. By reflecting, one could access information that would provide even the smallest degree of clarity to any circumstance given that they are open to receiving it. And so, our innate gift of curiosity prompts us to use our higher thinking skills and reflect on certain aspects we find within us, serving as a vital instrument for human progress and development. This is important because we might be in a time where the advancement of our species—in terms of thriving potential— depends more on the depth and quality of our thoughts rather than our pursuit of material success. *"But what if it's also predestined that I am not receptive to what I find within me in my introspective journey?"* Then it is what it is. But there was still something that prompted you to seek. So, what's that about? When people lose this feeling, they become severe nihilists and slowly but surely deteriorate. There's something quite special about our curiosity and sense of wonder.

Whether or not free will exists, we must continue to exert effort in making the most out of every situation by executing the most wholesome choices one can manage, aimed at making matters better rather than worse. Yet, once these decisions are made, we must also learn to accept/surrender to their outcomes by cultivating the idea that perhaps whatever ends up unfolding for us was bound to happen.

The word "surrender", as noted in a previous chapter, might elicit uncomfortable emotions, and cause the misinterpretation of the word particularly in Western culture, where it is often equated with relinquishing control and yielding to other's authority, resulting in perceived weakness and vulnerability to exploitation. However, in the Eastern perspective, surrendering is usually interpreted as aligning with a higher power, such as the will of God. I want to clarify that surrendering does not mean giving up; rather, it means we may continue in our efforts without becoming disheartened when circumstances deviate from our expectations.

As previously mentioned, with the concepts of "determinism" and "fatalism" sadly there will exist individuals who take advantage and abuse the idea of "surrender" by using divine authority as another justification for harmful actions, thereby casting doubt on the value of surrender. Considering this viewpoint emphasizes the usefulness and benefits of governmental systems. These systems establish and enforce regulations to prevent such abuses and mitigate unnecessary suffering.

"If men were angels, no government would be necessary." – James Madison

While instances of misconduct still occur with governmental systems already in practice, it is commonly believed that without these structures in place, such occurrences would be even more widespread. The truth is that complete surrender doesn't happen on its own or spontaneously. Those who are ready to genuinely surrender to the will of God[2], have also acquired the wisdom to understand the significance of their decisions since they have cultivated a profound comprehension of the underlying unity and operations of existence—an aspect many can remain blind to for many lifetimes. What was once a fragmented and divided identity has now become reintegrated, not only within themselves but also across various levels of reality. They have come to realize how every living entity is interconnected into a meticulously organized and cohesive whole, therefore they grasp that causing harm to others is essentially equivalent to harming themselves.

> 2. I, personally, don't find it necessary to anthropomorphize God. I am content referring to God without fully grasping its existential nature or profound depth. I also do not need scientific evidence of its existence, since I have a strong feeling that it is everything and everywhere, all and nothing, no word can capture what it is. *"The kingdom of God is inside you and all around you"*—Gospel of Thomas.

Chapter V. A Universal Longing

There is a wonderful wise old man I enjoy listening to, who brings me instant peace and comfort as soon as I hear him speak. This man's name is John Butler, a British author who shares his wisdom gained from years of dedicated daily prayer and meditation, highlighting the significance of staying rooted in reality of the present moment, by keeping our *"feet on the ground"*, as he often says.

I will never forget the day he asked one of the most humble questions I've ever heard someone ask: *"What can I give you that you haven't already got?"*. He believes each of us has at our disposal all we could ever want; we are complete. However, this is an important aspect of our life that we have not been taught how to access but also goes against everything we have been led to believe. *"If everything we need is within us, why do we seek meaningful connections with others?",* I asked myself. What I've come to find is that our love or friendship towards others has usually been of the conditional sort— I scratch your back, you scratch mine type of relationship. Where as long as they avoid certain behaviors, they will continue to receive our love or support. However, if they betray us in any manner, we feel justified in closing off our hearts to them unless they make amends for their mistakes.

Truth is, it is our *sense of identity*, or The Ego, that experiences disturbance, humiliation, foolishness, betrayal, resentment, and more. Our soul remains untouched by these experiences because the soul is part of something that is so unimaginably vast, incomprehensibly wise, and loving. We just have never been taught how to tap into this inner "completeness", "wisdom", or "love" (not sure how to define it) fully, except through occasional glimpses provided by external influences like other individuals, substances, events, music, and so on— some of these experiences offer us a more profound access to this place inside us where the completeness resides, so to speak.

It's a funny dynamic really if we look at the great example pointed out by Ram Dass when he explained that once we find the individual that is our doorway to that place inside us where we feel full, complete, or as we often say: "loved", we don't want to lose that access and so we marry them that way we keep them near for the rest of our lives. Isn't that interesting? It's absolutely hilarious because we know he's not wrong.

When this individual no longer helps us reach that place inside us, that's when problems arise, leading to increased arguments and often culminating in the dissolution of the relationship in search of someone else who can reignite that connection within us. This pattern repeats for many individuals. Of course, not all switch partners but instead seek alternative ways to fill this void, often resorting to activities with less moral implications such as thrill-seeking adventures, shopping, gambling, or certain substances to give us that much-needed jolt— we become junkies in a way. This perpetual quest for external validation (or love) stems from the misconception that what we yearn for is to be found strictly outside of ourselves, leading to a never-ending pursuit of satisfaction; a perpetual loop as symbolized by the ancient Ouroboros. A symbol found in various early civilizations such as the ancient Egyptians, Greeks, Amazonians, and others, that depicts a snake (or dragon) devouring its own tail. Though Ouroboros is mostly used to represent the continual cycle of destruction and re-birth, I am using it in this context since I find its visual representation useful and applicable.

This is why we are in the constant *chase* for external gratification —something marketing professionals exploit in highly sophisticated ways— and it can be quite maddening because at what point will it be enough? It often takes a significant level of frustration to prompt one to seek internal fulfillment and finally put an end to this cycle.

> *"Our hearts are restless until we rest in thee."*— St. Augustine

Now, I do not mean to imply that we would stop or that it is pointless to form meaningful relationships with others, on the contrary, having this understanding can enhance the depth and authenticity of relationships, provided that all parties involved share a similar perspective. "W*hat if they don't?* you might wonder. Well…that's where we roll up our sleeves and the most meaningful work we'll ever do begins because this presents us with a situation that doesn't align with our ideals, and thus, tests our patience, compassion, and empathy. The path we take from thereon will depend on how much pain, discomfort, annoyance, or frustration we are willing to tolerate while we work on the situation at hand. Better yet, how much are we willing to *sacrifice* to reach ultimate liberation?

[Side note: Ultimate liberation lies in realizing we are already complete. Nothing can touch the soul; the soul is not bothered. "Samantha" certainly gets bothered. "Samantha" gets angry. "Samantha" gets depressed. But that's not all "Samantha" is. "Samantha" knows that when she closes her eyes, and takes a deep breath, she can go within her where she can find the source of endless fulfillment.]

If you happen to be dealing with a complete "*rat butler*" –a term my 7-year-old son recently used to instill offense, which I found utterly hilarious and highly creative— what we usually do is, we will attempt to persuade those involved to adopt our perspective, aligning with what we perceive as the correct course of action. While our viewpoint may indeed be right, they cannot see or refuse to see this because it threatens their ego but beware because this can very quickly transform into a power struggle between the egos, and one must be careful not to see others from a superior stance of righteousness just because they happen to understand aspects of existence that other's continue struggling to grasp— one must always keep the door open to the possibility of being wrong and remembering that in the end they too, do not know it all. On top of that, if you are indeed facing a "rat butler", take a moment to see what they might be reflecting to you? Is there a lack of gratefulness on our end that we are potentially forgetting? Or are we acting in ways that we are currently asking them not to act towards us?

Now, sometimes we truly have done nothing wrong, and we could be entirely right. But still… I find that even this wonderful feeling of "being right" must not remain. We need to let that one go also. Let it go. I know it causes uneasiness, and I cannot explain how or why it is that it works, but it somehow does.

Nevertheless, the individual that holds such a deeper understanding must take responsibility and practice what they know, this begins by stepping back from the ego-driven conflict and instead engage with the essence of the other person, appealing to their soul rather than their ego. This task becomes more challenging if they are unwilling to momentarily set aside their ego for the sake of harmony. However, recognizing it as merely the ego asserting itself can lessen the impact of such difficult interactions. A way to do this begins by cultivating a special kind of awareness, where you build a sort of buffer between you and the other person or the situation, but you continue to be present, you just stop taking yourself so seriously. Once one gets really good at this (I am still but a mere apprentice) we will eventually have no problem allowing other's ego to have their ego trip. At times we may indeed need to step away, or say "no", but will not take it as personally as we once did and will continue to love them regardless.

Chapter VI. Layers of Reality

One evening, as I sat in my backyard under the night sky, I found myself lost in contemplation while gazing at the fire flickering in the nearby firepit and the candles I had lit for the occasion. It felt as though I was in nature's own living room. This evening held a special significance for me as I aimed to access a realm that is usually difficult to access due to our hectic daily lives and fast-paced routines.

Once arrived at this deep introspective state, I was presented with a visual of life unfolding like a wardrobe of costumes passing before my eyes, with each piece of garment symbolizing different experiences such as circumstances, individuals, ideas, or beliefs. It was hard to determine whether these "clothes" (representing events, people, ideas, and beliefs) came to us or if we were the ones who sought them out. Regardless, we invariably find ourselves wearing these "clothes"—in other words, experiencing events, encountering people, adopting beliefs and ideas.

This imagery provided me with what felt like the direct experience I needed to understand something I already knew about but had not quite sunk in. In other words, I knew the theory aspect of it, but was missing the experience/practice. And so, the thought that stemmed from this was that we have the tendency to hold on to things in our lives so remarkably tight, sometimes to the point of causing our own suffocation (digging ourselves further into a hole of depression, anxiety, anger…), and when we sense the threat that it will be taken away we hold on to it even tighter, we usually do this with people or our material acquisitions (refusing to take that piece of clothing off).

      Furthermore, our physical forms, and consequently, the identities shaped by them over time, are temporary and do not entirely define us. Put simply, we are not our body, occupation, income, wardrobe, or achievements. While they may currently reflect aspects of ourselves and carry a certain amount of value/significance in one dimension of reality, they still only represent but a fraction of who we say we are, and even that fraction is not permanent.

      So, each role we play on this Earth, in a way shapes how we perceive our reality. If you've noticed, when we wear our "parent" hats, we will perceive the world through different lenses than when we are wearing our "employee" hats. But also, when all is well in our life, we see the world through a comparatively different lens than when everything is going side-ways, all of a sudden, the people in our lives are tyrannical, our homes are smaller than ever, the imperfections stand out and it's all just plain inefficient as can be. We can become very different under different circumstances. For instance, in the past I would become quite a mean person after going long hours without food. However, now that I've incorporated fasting into my lifestyle, I no longer have this reaction.

What I'm trying to say is that we exhibit different personas at various moments. Therefore, we can shift our perspective to serve our needs, but it's up to us to decide what outcome we want. But also: *Who is leading?* Which "you", out of the many fragmentations that have developed through time (the sub-identities), which "you" is engaging with the present reality? Therefore, we cannot ask what is externally real any more than we can identify the truest part of ourselves– this is a hard one to understand but also to explain.

Nonetheless, each layer of reality fulfills its distinct purpose, much like the various layers within ourselves serve their unique functions. Nonetheless, while they are all beneficial, knowing precisely when to utilize them isn't something we always succeed in.

This, of course, also applies to our beliefs since our beliefs guide a substantial portion of our actions but still only reflect but a portion of who, or what, we inherently are since. Each of us maintains specific beliefs that we cherish because they offer some utility. As previously noted, beliefs typically align with either scientific principles or mystical ideologies, which greatly influence our everyday experiences. It is essential to view these beliefs as temporary means that move us toward uncovering forgotten truths about our inherent selves and what we're here to do. Rather than becoming fixated on them indefinitely, thereby tethering ourselves to belief systems and inhibiting true freedom, we should use them to move closer to the profound self-discovery we yearn for. This might entail the consideration of what all religions have to say and not just one in particular. This also means not holding on so tightly to the data provided by science but also considering the mystical aspects of life that remain obscure or misunderstood, and vice versa.

You may be thinking how audacious it is for me to suggest that everyone shares this particular yearning. And indeed, you're correct... perhaps I am mistaken. There's a significant probability (50%) that everything I've mentioned so far are mere whimsical thoughts. So, let's play along with them in that light and see where they take us.

In any case, I suspect that there exists within all of us a longing for the Truth. This arises from my own observations on how many individuals incessantly pursue hollow substitutes—external sources for meaningful connection and validation, both of which are usually given conditionally.

Many have ceased their quest for God, while others have entirely abandoned their belief in a higher power. Now, I won't delve into the beliefs of non-believers, but I can speak to those who still hold faith and have only stopped actively seeking it—as I've been in that position. This can often be attributed to the overwhelming focus on meeting societal demands, many of which we have mistakenly internalized as our own, serving as a subtle and clever tactic to retain a sense of control. These demands keep us with constant expectations breathing down our necks, draining our energy. This struggle is particularly evident in urban lifestyles, where schedules leave hardly any room to just sit back and smell the roses. Instead, any free time available is often spent seeking instant gratification to make the most out of this brief down-time they have before having to delve back into the relentless cycle of productivity. This cycle can be incredibly exhausting and leaves little space for spiritual contemplation or growth.

However, I've observed a common belief that if our external circumstances were more favorable, we would have the time to engage in meditation, prayer, or reconnect with our spirituality. What I've come to understand is that God is always present, and it only requires us to mentally reestablish that connection even if it's right in the middle of life's chaos. Accessing the inner realm tied to higher awareness is *not* a privilege reserved for a chosen few. There's no need to retreat to a monastery, sit alone in darkness for extended periods, or practice yoga in exotic locations. Many lack such luxuries and have no other choice but to confront their circumstances head-on. In other words, cultivating a spiritual connection doesn't demand wealth, social status, or extensive time commitments.

In fact, it has happened to several people that their most profound revelations and transformations occurred precisely at a time when their lives were far from ideal. Every difficulty can serve as an opportunity to see things from a perspective that doesn't take the ego so seriously. Look at it as a game, if you must, you are a character playing a role but within you lies something that can never be disturbed and holds incredible power. When we can truly recognize this, we are capable of such wonderful acts of kindness we didn't know we had in us. More importantly:

"You'll be able to stand in the fire and not get burned"— Ram Dass

A detail to always keep in mind, however, is that individuals vary in their capacity to endure challenges due to their unique circumstances and reasons. Ultimately, their life is a deeply personal journey, and it's unfair to judge anyone based on their tolerance levels. I believe that each person does their best given their abilities, which are influenced by their current level of awareness and personal evolution.

Chapter VII. Stop Grabbing

Many will go on the path of enlightenment with the aim of transcending the ego and reaching eternal nirvana. However, some view this as a passive way of avoiding life's challenges—a form of detachment that keeps them at a distance from life. And this is true. If the spiritual or religious journey is done with the wrong intention, this wrong intention is usually concealed due to reluctance to admit that behind it are ego-driven desires for status, recognition, or praise. I have noticed this tendency frequently in Western cultures, especially when such pursuits remain trendy. Therefore, when approached without genuine and humble intentions on this path, individuals face the risk of self-deception. They may not be aware that they have fallen into yet another trap, as the ego constantly sets many traps to evade its own death. However, if approached correctly and with a willingness to relinquish the ego (to undergo ego death, so to speak), you will be less fearful when it is time to shed the body and experience a physical death. A way to tell how serious they are about this pursuit is by looking at the way they react towards difficult people or situations. It is easy to be kind, compassionate, and understanding towards people we feel so fond of, but what about when this is not the case? This is when it's most important to shed the ego, when it's most challenging to do so. Of course, we might continue to deviate, and we won't always get it right, but we can always reflect and make a better attempt in the future.

The reality is that when one can free themselves from the control, demands, and greed of the ego, they will find themselves quite comfortable right where they are and as they are. The constant need for "more" and "better" will not have such a grip on them anymore. They continue to engage with life and people in beautifully meaningful ways, they will continue to pursue dreams and aspirations and honor their given roles, as mother, wife, friend, daughter, etc… but they learn to *"stop grabbing"*, as Alan Watts puts it.

Chapter VIII. Abstract Ripples

We've all heard the popular phrase: "*Karma is a *itch*", I disagree. Karma is impartial and thus fair.

Once one begins to pay closer attention, one cannot help but notice the interconnectedness of events, and with even further and brutally honest examination of the paths each of us has trotted, we can surely uncover the ways in which we have ended up right where we are. However, I also recognize that not all will be as clear, cut, and dry. Some of these will perhaps carry on from past lifetimes or could be due to transgenerational trauma which could explain the obscurity of some of the experiences or emotional knots that seem to have happened out of nowhere with no obvious causation one can put their finger on. With that said, and if the law of cause and effect follows us through indefinitely, then what remains unresolved in this lifetime will present itself yet again in the future, until it is brought back to *equilibrium*—not necessarily right or wrong, but merely seeking balance. This idea may seem improbable to the average logician, to think that it's just my mind playing tricks on me, creating patterns that do not exist, which is entirely possible and a fair point. However, I choose to hold onto this unconventional idea and treat it seriously in the event that it is true.

The ultimate form of freedom awaits those who are willing to make the most profound sacrifice: *themselves*. It's been pointed out by several sages that once one can let go of everything; it is then that they will attain it all. However, this requires a great deal of trust, or faith…

> *"Faith, is where you let go, not where you hold on"*— Alan Watts

But before we can go into that process of liberation, we need to mentally retrace our steps in order to find out more about ourselves— you need to have a good grasp of who you are on this planet in order to know what you're attempting to let go of, otherwise how could you let go if you don't know what you're holding on to?

Among many things that will come up, we will invariably come across the times where our hypocrisy took centerstage, or where we've caused unnecessary suffering instead of offering compassion, or the times when pride hindered our ability to admit our errors, or the occasions where selfishness was needed but withheld.

I have a feeling that mere internal recognition of these shortcomings isn't enough; true liberation demands not only honest admission but also outward expression of these acknowledgments; a sort of purging, so to speak. Of course, this requires courage because our ego sees itself severely compromised when these sorts of reflections appear. Nevertheless, it is still beneficial since it encourages us to move toward a higher level of awareness, and closer to our true nature, and thus, God. While this path doesn't guarantee infallibility, the frequency of missteps does tend to diminish as individuals come to grips with the realization that their suffering often stems from the suffering they've inflicted on others, be it consciously or subconsciously. Once this realization dawns on you, excuses suddenly disappear, and self-deception becomes almost impossible. Before you know it, every interaction with others reflects, or mirrors, back to us what we couldn't or wouldn't see before. So, we're at a crossroads: one leads to acknowledge this truth sincerely or the other path is to deny, rationalize, and evade it which holds the seeds of our own pain down the road, all we are ultimately doing is postponing it. If this is the case, revert to Part I, and start all over.

Attempting to outsmart the profound wisdom of nature is futile. No one eludes the consequences of their actions indefinitely, no matter how seemingly insignificant they may appear at first. As I mentioned in the topic of free will, how even the smallest details had a significant impact on shaping my current circumstances. There is no escape from accountability. Whether we acknowledge it or not, whether we recognize the interconnectedness of all things or remain blind to it, the universe unfailingly balances the scales of justice. Thus, let us tread mindfully upon the path of life, leading with the heart.

Chapter IX. Suffering is Grace

I would not have been able to arrive at what I have been able to understand now if it weren't for the insight of many, though one of them stands out more than the rest. Let me share a brief personal anecdote.

When I was 22 years old, I developed friendships that introduced me to a different world. A world quite frankly, not as different from the weird ones I had already visited, usually of the esoteric sort from my teenage years— I found them intriguing. In any case, these individuals were the first to tell me about the existence of psychedelics and the great names that used these as tools for entering altered states of consciousness in order to extract meaningful insights that offer greater clarity into aspects of life, the sort that provoke much curiosity.

The name Ram Dass was mentioned and one of his most popular published works was handed over to me, a book titled '*Be Here, Be Now*'. I remember reading the book and being incredibly drawn to the level of eccentricity Ram Dass decided to style his words, it was quite the trip actually, perhaps that was his intention. I knew the book was loaded with wise words but could not understand them profoundly, therefore I didn't make much of it.

By the way, Ram Dass, formerly known as Richard Alpert, was once a professor of clinical psychology at Harvard University. During his time there, he crossed paths with another clinical psychologist, Timothy Leary. Together, they embarked on a journey of experimentation and research involving psychedelics such as LSD and psilocybin. Their aim was not only to explore the psychological effects of these substances but also to gain deeper insights into human consciousness in general. Their efforts to sustain this admirable endeavor were brief because they faced several controversies stemming from the uncharted territory and fear it evoked in less curious or adventurous minds at the time. Yet, Ram Dass's influence continued to grow, particularly after his transformative experiences in India where he met his guru, Neem Karoli Baba, also known as "Maharaj-ji,", later returning to the West with great wisdom and teachings that continues to live within many individual's minds and hearts.

Moving on...

I had my first psychedelic experience back then, at the age of 22. I was given mushrooms for this, and I was fortunate that my first experience was with these people since they approached psychedelics with respect and not as a source for fun—which set the precedent for me from thereon. Long story short, once the effect began to wear off, I remember clearly saying: *"Everyone needs to try this. We need to find a way to put it in the water or something"*, because it's a necessary boundary dissolution, in other words, a necessary Ego death. When one can temporarily shed their ego, they are able to recognize the totality that exists within them.

Before I continue, I do not recommend trying psychoactive substances for the first time in any of these cases: alone, near a large body of water, access to a balcony, at a party or large gathering. Stick to the sort that have a history of shamanic usage instead of the synthetic sort. Quite frankly have no interest in any others since I find psilocybin to be usually gentle in its delivery, at least with me. Additionally, it is crucial to pay attention to the *"set and setting"*[1] – a concept developed by Ram Dass, Timothy Leary and Ralph Metzner and one that was mentioned in their book 'Psychedelic Experience: A Manual Based on the Tibetan Book of the Dead'.

1. Set and setting— means your state of mind right before using psychedelics, and it is just as important as the people/environment in which it will be experienced in.

However, this is also something quite important... as ethnobiologist, Terence Mckenna, another individual highly curious about the psychedelic world, once wisely said (this was extracted from a recording):

"If you're fearful already and fighting to keep from being overwhelmed by confusion at what's going on in your life at the paper box factory or something, then probably tossing in mega doses of hallucinogens is not the way for you to do it" ... *"I don't want to make it sound like it's absolutely riskless. Physically, I think it's pretty safe unless you are odd in some way, but you need to know this. You know? You don't want to find out you're odd an hour and a half into it"*... *"If you are delicately balanced, if your whole life has been about* (nervously) *not looking at that or that or that, then this is <u>not</u> your game"*.

Many years passed. Friendships dissolved; new ones emerged. Major changes happened. I fell off the track— momentarily. Until one day, perhaps only a couple of years ago, a quote from Ram Dass caught my attention. *"Hey, I know that name,"* I thought. Suddenly I found myself looking up more quotes from Ram Dass, then found more of his literary work and I just could not stop reading and listening to what he had to share. I got it. However, this took me many years of introspection (some with mushrooms), suffering, reading, observing... Ever since my reencounter with Ram Dass, I have been using him as my guide since then and has played a major role in my ability to understand what I am trying to share with others now. I couldn't have done it without him. Or maybe not as quickly... definitely not as quickly.

Here is more of what I've been able to draw from all of it:

> To be alive means one is bound to immense pleasure but also great suffering.

Not many individuals seem inclined to engage in "the work", or "shadow work" as Freud would have put it, necessary for personal growth and understanding. Rather than focusing on our own growth, we often instead seek to mold others (or situations) to fit our expectations and preferences. When this endeavor proves fruitless, we resort to shutting them out, either through passive withdrawal or aggressive confrontation, or both. After all, addressing our shortcomings and taking responsibility for our actions can be far too arduous, leading us to prefer blame-shifting over the difficult task of introspection and personal accountability.

As Ram Dass insightfully observed and pointed out; we are drawn to the drama of life, our own *"melodrama."* Yes, this includes anxiety, trauma, and depression—because without it, who would we blame? What would we complain, fight, or cry about? It's no fun to blame ourselves, or worse yet... to have absolutely no one to blame and simply drop it, drop the anger, the depression, the anxiety—that's insane, we can't just drop it! Or can we?

Ram Dass also frequently emphasizes how suffering is grace and uses a strong example such as pointing out the expressed discomfort many feel at the portrayal of Jesus on the cross in churches, interpreting it as an unnecessary and brutal reminder of the evil inflicted upon such a person and the tragedy of this event, and instead offers a different perspective on this by highlighting that Jesus endured such agony not only for us but also as an example of the profound comprehension a human being can achieve of the inseparability of grace and suffering. He suggests that Jesus exhibited what it looks like to arrive at such a level of understanding even amidst profound suffering, therefore one should take the image of Jesus on the cross as a symbolic representation or as a reminder that we too, possess the capacity to face such adversities by cultivating a deeper understanding of life.

Practicing this can progressively reduce our tendency to become reactive toward negative experiences, as well as dropping resentment, bitterness, anger, or depression. Eventually one takes all the events in their lives as another opportunity to step closer in this direction— the direction of realizing what our work in this life is about, and not attaching ourselves too deeply to our given identity, or character, in this realm of reality while still enjoying the ride and being of use when use is needed.

Lastly, nothing has drawn me, and many others, closer to God than the moments where great suffering was experienced. Suffering is a profound gift since each moment of suffering gives us the chance to reach out and reconnect with God. How, then, could we ever see suffering as unnecessary?

> *"Whoever finds the interpretation of these sayings will not experience death." –*
> Gospel of Thomas

Last Thought

When we zoom in, things matter... a lot. But isn't it interesting that the further we step back from it all, the initial importance we place on these things gradually diminishes, and eventually loses its power? It suddenly all becomes beautiful, and simple because we realize that it's just life happening as it naturally should.

And this, ladies and gentlemen, concludes the introduction.

In a quiet room filled with the soft glow of candlelight, a young writer sat at their desk, pen poised over a blank page. Thoughts swirled within. "I wonder if I will read what I am writing now in another life?" they whispered, "will I remember it was me who wrote it?".

As the words took shape, a strange sensation washed over them—a feeling of déjà vu tinged with uncertainty.

"Just as I have read from others and their work resonated with me", the writer pondered, "was I perhaps one of them in the past and have found my own work yet again?"

"Perhaps there is more to this life than met the eye", the writer thought.

As the writer closed the journal, there was a feeling of childlike wonder. Maybe someday, in another life, the writer would indeed read these words again and would find answers that at one point eluded the writer in previous lifetimes. Until then, the writer would continue to leave behind a trail of testaments filled with thoughts and emotions for its future self to discover.

Printed in Great Britain
by Amazon